A-MAZE-ING MAP Mysteries

by Holly Kowitt

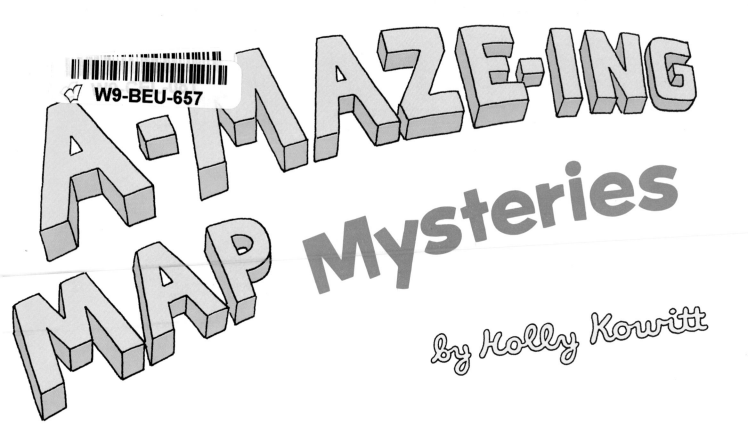

SCHOLASTIC INC.

New York   Toronto   London   Auckland   Sydney

ISBN 0-590-48083-9

12 11 10 9 8 7 6 5 4 3 2   6 7 8 9/9 0/0
Printed in the U.S.A.   14
First Scholastic printing, May 1995

For Julia Rose

Mystery
of the
Haunted Town

Pleasantville looks like an ordinary town.
But Jimmy and Maria realize something is very
wrong when their car runs out of gas and they
look for help. Not only are most of the roads
blocked, but the town is completely deserted!
Can you help them find the only possible route
to a gas station so they can escape this
haunted town forever?

Mystery of the Haunted House

The Harvey Mansion has been boarded up for years, and new neighbors Cindy and Tom have been warned to stay away. Some people say there's a ghost in the attic who wants to be set free! Five keys are hidden around the house. But only one key unlocks the attic door. Use the clues below to find which of the five keys is the one that will set the ghost free at last. It's hidden in a room with the following things in it:

a treasure chest
a chandelier
a chair
a staircase
a painting

Circle the right key!

Julie's Backyard

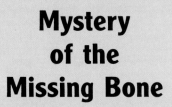

Mystery
of the
Missing Bone

Julie's dad is a famous scientist who travels the
world to dig up dinosaur bones. He can't wait
to show Julie his newest discovery, but when
he opens his briefcase, the bone is gone.
The culprit must be Crackers, the family dog.
He loves to bury bones in the backyard.

Look at the map of Julie's backyard to find out
where Crackers buries his bones. Then follow
the directions below to uncover the real
dinosaur bone!

Crackers leaves the house from the screen door
and stops to rest on the red welcome mat,
then he heads:

1 square south to pull up some tomato plants.
5 squares east to chew on a badminton birdie.
7 squares south to drink from the kiddie pool.
4 squares west to check his mailbox.
4 squares north to nap under the bench.
1 square west to jump in the pond.
3 squares south to swim.
He buries his bone in the same square.

Circle the dinosaur bone.

Mystery
of the
Lost Loot

The Grunge Gang is the terror of Culpepper
County! They stole a sack full of gold from
the miners at Culpepper Creek and hid it
somewhere in this ghost town. In fact, they hid
it so well, they forgot where they put it! Is the
gold stashed in a stone chimney, a church
cupola, a teepee, a stagecoach, or a bag of
seeds? Use the clues below to find out.

The gold is north of the bank.
The gold is south of the dance hall.
The gold is east of the school.
The gold is west of the hotel.
Where is the gold?

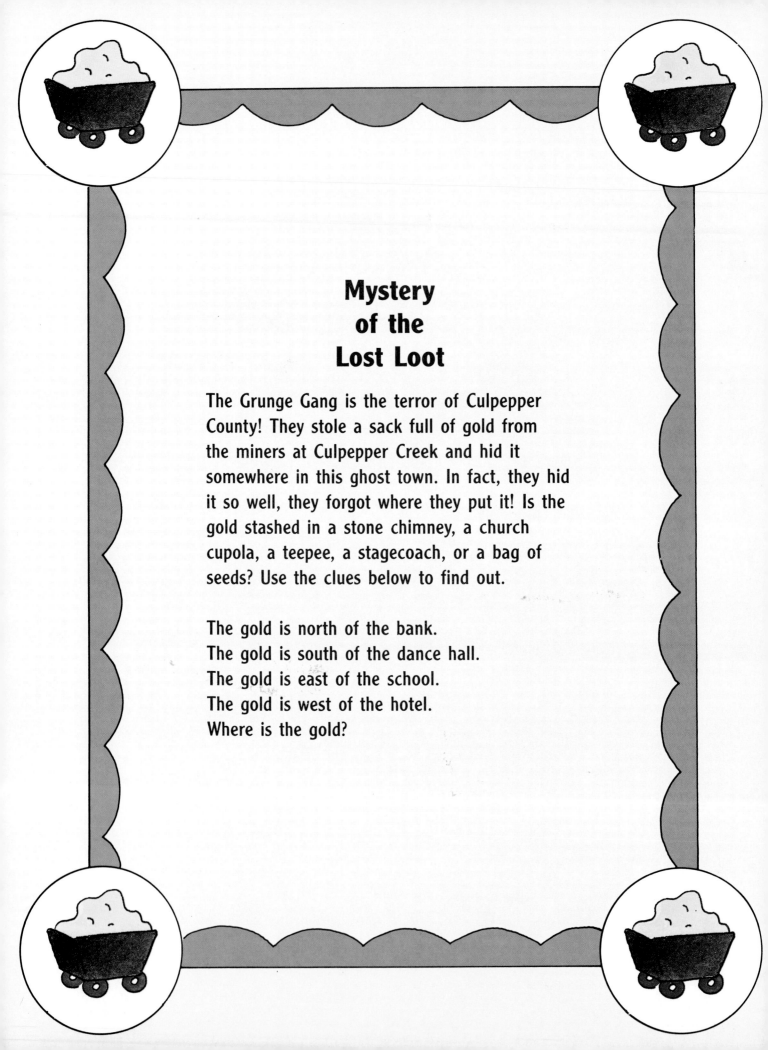

Town of Gooseburg

Mystery
of the
Lost Coins

Absentminded Mr. Spacey was bringing his collection of rare coins to the Gooseburg Town Museum. But, first, he stopped at the Astroburger for a bite to eat. He mistakenly paid for his corn dog and root beer with some priceless ancient coins! Ned, the cashier at Astroburger, passed the coins along to Barney, another customer, as change. Use the directions below to follow Barney around town. Each time you pass a letter, put it in the space below to find the location of the lost coins.

Barney began at the Astroburger, then walked:

2 blocks south past the trailer court.
2 blocks west past the movie theater.
5 blocks north past the garden.
1 block east, 1 block south, and 2 blocks east past the lake.
2 blocks south to the city park.

wishing well

Mystery of the Hidden Sea Monster

Lake Eerie can be a spooky place, especially at night. That's when local fishermen spotted an empty boat speeding along — with no driver! People say there's a sea monster who visits the lake every hundred years, but no one knows what he looks like. Follow the numbered dots described below and you will have a picture of the sea monster's face. Then find him hiding on the map and circle him.

Start at the sunken ship and travel:
southeast to the submarine.
northeast to the seaplane.
southeast to the houseboat.
northeast to the garbage barge.
southeast to the floating bathtub.
northeast to the dragon.

Draw a circle around the volcano and the island with the palm tree. Now see if you can find the sea monster hiding around the lake.

Mystery
of the
Green Slime

It started out like any normal day in Beanster, Indiana. Then, suddenly, a mysterious green slime began to spread throughout the town! No one knows where it came from, but Slim and his Slimebusters are determined to find out. They just received an anonymous note with instructions to find the source of this gruesome green stuff!

Start at the school in the south of town and then go:

west just past the playground.
north past the movie theater.
east across the bridge.
north past the castle and the toy store.
west across the second bridge to the
  gas station.
south past the diner and the hat store.

Turn east to find the source of the green slime.

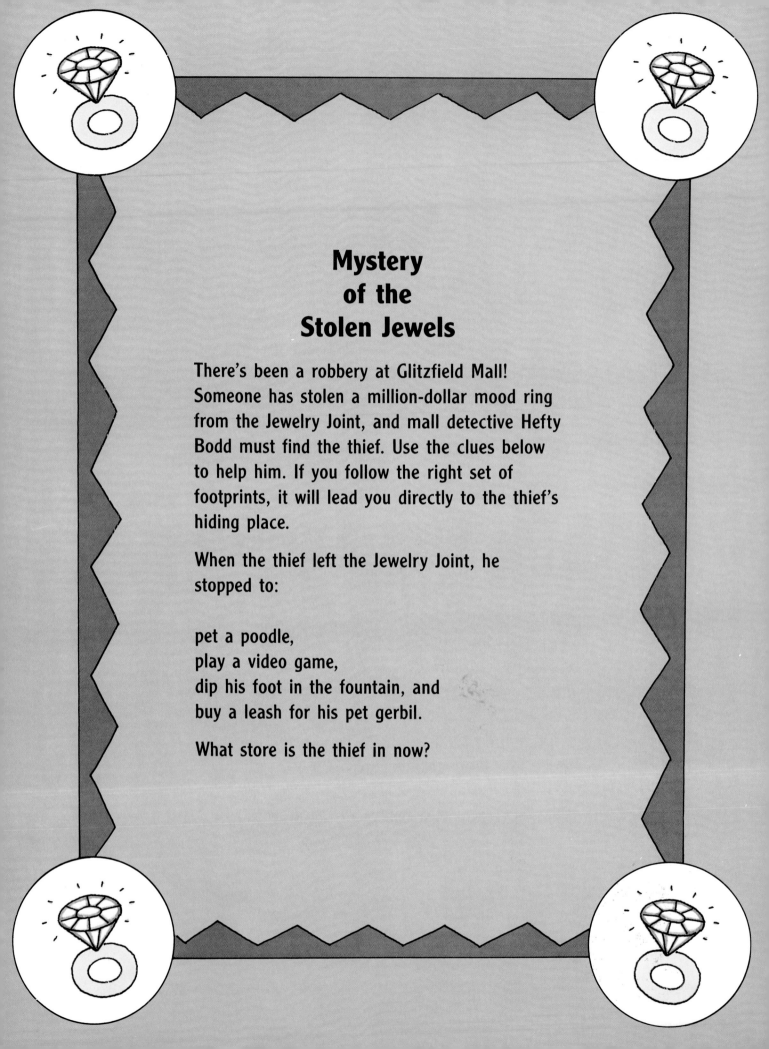

Mystery of the Stolen Jewels

There's been a robbery at Glitzfield Mall! Someone has stolen a million-dollar mood ring from the Jewelry Joint, and mall detective Hefty Bodd must find the thief. Use the clues below to help him. If you follow the right set of footprints, it will lead you directly to the thief's hiding place.

When the thief left the Jewelry Joint, he stopped to:

pet a poodle,
play a video game,
dip his foot in the fountain, and
buy a leash for his pet gerbil.

What store is the thief in now?

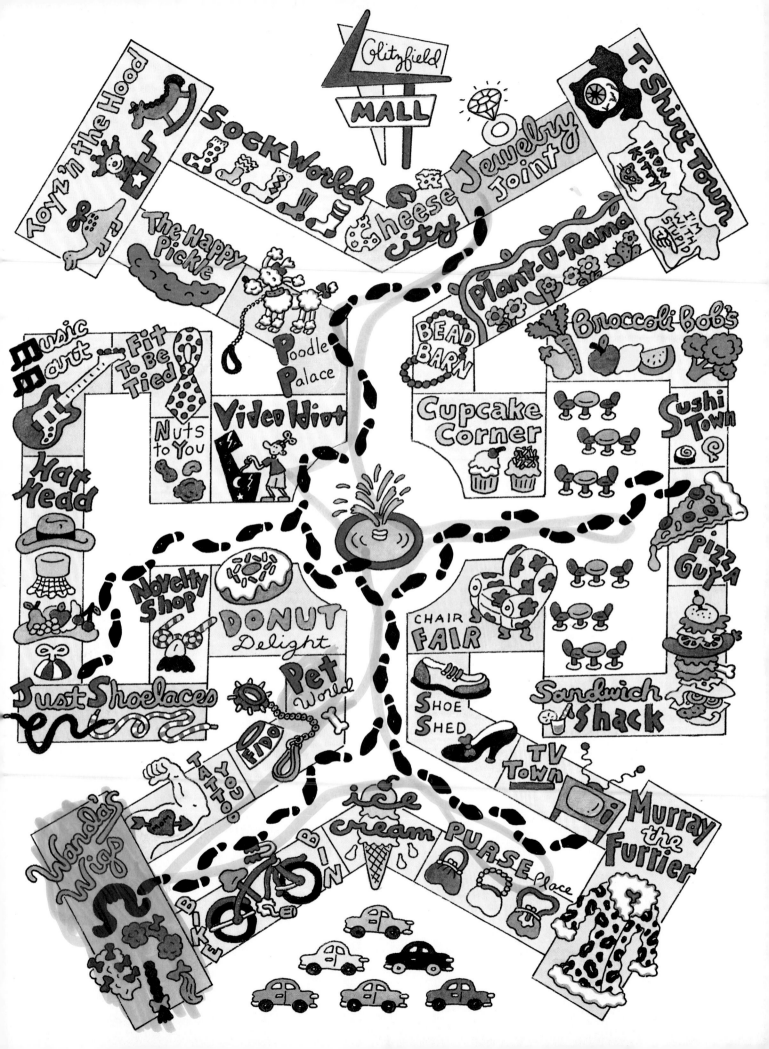

Star Island

Mystery of the Buried Treasure

Everyone says that Star Island used to be a home to pirates! One day Randy finds a bottle on the beach. Inside the bottle is a map and a note, telling him how to find a treasure chest! The map has many "X's" on it, but only one "X" stands for the buried treasure. Can you find it?

Begin at the big anchor (5-C) and go:

west to the plank and cross over the alligators (5-B).
north to the snake pit (4-B).
west to the hut (4-A).
north to the dinosaur skeleton (3-A).
east to the monkey in the tree and north to the cave (3-B).
north to the swamp (B-1).
east to the graveyard (C-1).
south to the snake around the tree (C-2).

The nearest "X" is the buried treasure.

Mystery of the Lost Dog

When Rudy's parents announce they're going on a fun-filled vacation, he knows he's in big trouble. This year's destination is Snookertown, Ohio, home of the World's Largest Paper Clip. At least Rudy's got his dog, Barky, with him... or so he thinks until they get to Snookertown, and Barky's nowhere to be found! Rudy must find his dog before the town dogcatcher finds him first!

Look at the two maps of Snookertown. The top map shows all the places in Snookertown where Barky could be hiding. Each place has a corresponding symbol on the map key. The bottom map is blank. Using the map key, draw the correct symbol on the blank map so the two maps look alike. We've done the first one for you.

One space on the blank map does not have a symbol in the map key. That's where Barky is hiding out.

SNOOKERTOWN

DINO WORLD 1

MOTEL

GREASE DOG
SOGGY FRIES
WATERY SHAKES

DINER
OUR FOOD IS THE WURST

GEORGE WASHINGTON SNEEZED HERE
ONLY 5⁰⁰

MINI GOLF KING

VIDEO Arcade

WEEDMORE PARK

TOWN DUMP

LAUNDERAMA

BURP 'N BOWL

BOWL

bad restaurant

dinosaur park

mini-golf course

picnic area

video games

garbage dump

Laundromat

motel

boring historical site

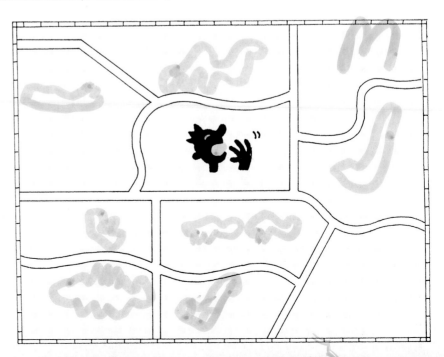

Mystery
of the
Underground
Caves

Steve is in for a surprise when he falls through a rabbit hole one day. Down below is a whole maze of underground caves! At the end of the maze is a locked door that reads KEEP OUT. What secret lurks behind the door? Use the clues below to follow the maze and help Steve find out. As you follow the directions, pick up letters along the way to discover the secret.

Go south past the sign.

Go east over the wooden plank to cross the
bubbling-green mud pool.

Continue east past the pile of bones, then
southeast toward the dinosaur fossil.

Go west past the pool of prehistoric fish.

Go southwest, then west under the
dripping ceiling.

Go south, then east past the ancient
cave paintings.

Continue east past the stalagmites to the
locked door.

GOLD MINE
_ _ _ _   _ _ _ _

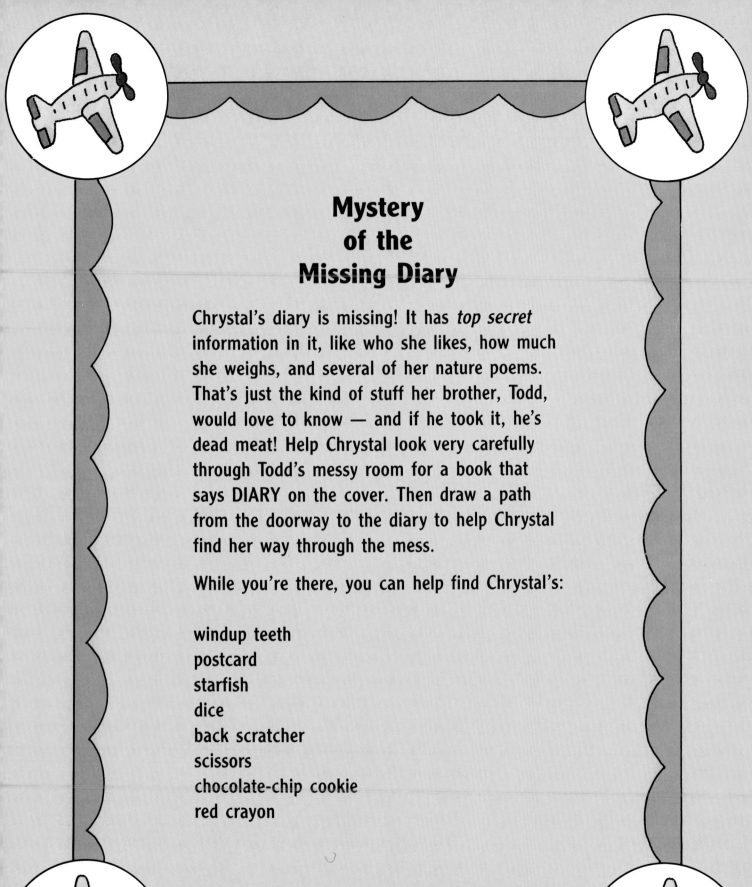

Mystery
of the
Missing Diary

Chrystal's diary is missing! It has *top secret* information in it, like who she likes, how much she weighs, and several of her nature poems. That's just the kind of stuff her brother, Todd, would love to know — and if he took it, he's dead meat! Help Chrystal look very carefully through Todd's messy room for a book that says DIARY on the cover. Then draw a path from the doorway to the diary to help Chrystal find her way through the mess.

While you're there, you can help find Chrystal's:

windup teeth
postcard
starfish
dice
back scratcher
scissors
chocolate-chip cookie
red crayon

Mystery
of the
Magic Locket

Lisa and Mitch are hiking at Wolf Woods. When they stop to rest on Skeleton Rock, Lisa finds a note with a secret message! The note says there's an antique necklace with a magic locket hidden in the hollow of an old oak tree. The trouble is, Wolf Woods is filled with old oak trees. Follow the path described in the note and help Lisa and Mitch find the tree with the locket inside.

Start at Skeleton Rock at the southwest corner
   of the woods, then go:
east, then south at the berry bush.
northeast at the swamp through the hollow log.
east at the dead tree.
north at the beehive.
west past the snake.
north at the mushroom path.
west at the mudslide to the water pump.
First tree south of the water pump has the
   magic locket.

WOLF WOODS

Make Your Own Map

Using the map key below, make your own classroom map. You can even make up some of your own symbols for other objects in your classroom.

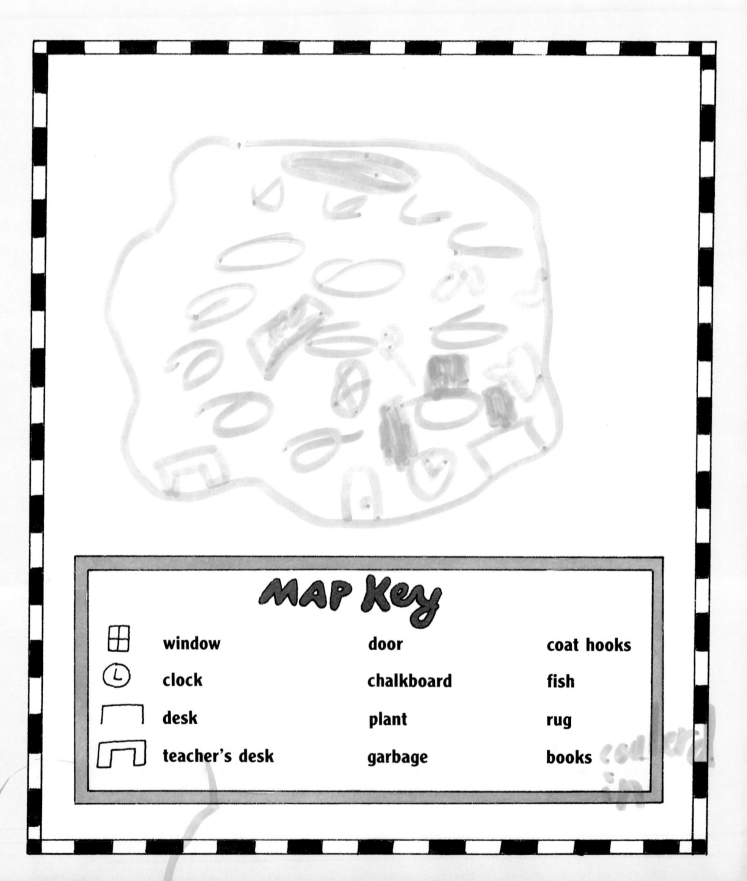

MAP Key

⊞	window	door	coat hooks
🕐	clock	chalkboard	fish
⊓	desk	plant	rug
⊓	teacher's desk	garbage	books

ANSWERS

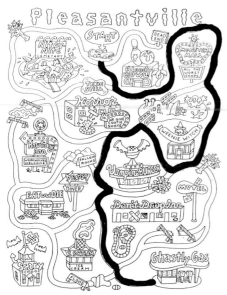

Pleasantville

Harvey House

Julie's Backyard

GHOST Town

Town of Gooseburg

WISHING WELL

Lake Eerie

Beanster, Indiana

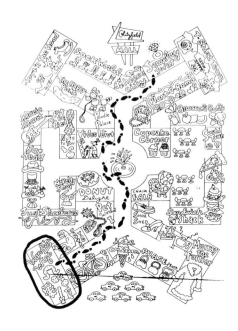

Star Island

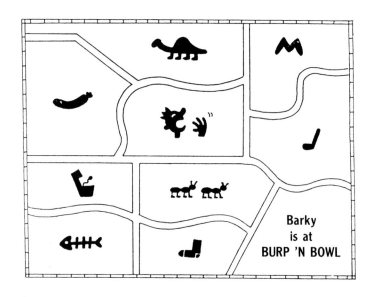

Barky
is at
BURP 'N BOWL

GOLD MINE

Todd's Room

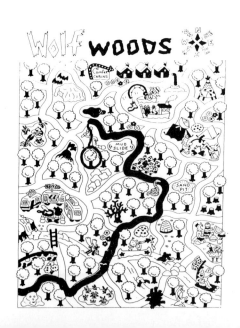

Wolf Woods